Just Here, Just Now

Also by R. H. W. Dillard

Poetry

The Day I Stopped Dreaming About Barbara Steele (1966)
News of the Nile (1971)
After Borges (1972)
The Greeting: New & Selected Poems (1981)

Fiction

The Book of Changes (1974)
The First Man on the Sun (1983)
Omniphobia (forthcoming)

Criticism

Horror Films (1976)
Understanding George Garrett (1988)

Just Here, Just Now

POEMS BY **R. H. W. Dillard**

> A token it is that time is precious: for God,
> that is geuer of tyme, geueth neuer to tymes
> to-geder, bot ich one after the other.
> — *The Clowde of Vnknowyng*

Louisiana State University Press

Baton Rouge and London   1994

Copyright © 1994 by R. H. W. Dillard
Manufactured in the United States of America
First printing
03 02 01 00 99 98 97 96 95 94   5 4 3 2 1

Designer: Amanda McDonald Key
Typeface: Bembo
Typesetter: G&S Typesetters, Inc.
Printer and binder: Thomson–Shore, Inc.

Library of Congress Cataloging-in-Publication Data
Dillard, R. H. W. (Richard H. W.), 1937–
    Just here, just now : poems / by R. H. W. Dillard.
        p.   cm.
    ISBN 0-8071-1919 (acid-free paper). — ISBN 0-8071-1920-2 (pbk.)
    PS3554.I4J87   1994
    811'.54—dc20   94-17830
                                                                 CIP

Some of these poems originally appeared in the following publications: *Chronicles; Denver Quarterly; Festival 88; New Virginia Review;* and *To Come Up and Grinning: A Tribute to George Garrett,* ed. Paul Ruffin and Stuart Wright (Huntsville, Tex., 1989).

Publication of this book has been supported by a grant from the National Endowment for the Arts in Washington, D.C., a federal agency.

For
Julia Johnson
&
Anita Thompson

It is like a breeze I have always felt,
Billowing out the silent curtains,
Bumping the pictures on the walls.
One day it is a warm breeze; one day, cold.
Today it is you.

Contents

Just Here, Just Now

Tips For a Traveler

In the Isle of Bananas,
The Republic of Fronds, you must
Always remember to sway with the wind,
Allow rages to pass into a whisper,
Bow your head before the blast
And wait for the approach of the eye.

In the Archipelago of Sky,
The Republic of Clouds, you must
Always remember to drift with the wind,
Skirt thunderheads with their ragged
Electric feet, thin out in sunlight
And flow across the moon all night.

In the Oberland of Height,
The Republic of Peaks, you must
Always remember to climb with the wind,
Cling to cragheads and sheets of stone,
Beware treacherous snows, seek shelter
When avalanches stumble from above.

In the Bower of Love,
The Republic of Amour, you must
Always remember to become the wind,
Expect constant surprise, suffer
The days to pass like turtles, the nights
To clang into explosions like prepared pianos.

In the Delta of Lianas,
The Republic of Rain, you must
Always remember to forget the wind,
To lie still in the moisture of your skin,
To bathe in the shadows of forgotten sunlight
Across a wide expanse of silent savannas.

for Julia Johnson

Fog at the Spa

Not the kittenish one you know
From the famous poem

Or the yellow fog
That darkened Eliot's heart

Or the coal-fired fogs
Of the books of our youth

Just this gray mist
That wisps through the balustrade

Floats the distant lake
Into the drifting sky

From the Norwegian *fogge*
Long grass on damp ground

Its blades brush Monique's shoulders
Bare under Maurice's jacket

She shivers as she feels herself
Sinking the tower with its clock

Sinking the steaming mineral springs
Sinking into the moist earth

Where everything is fog
And they are lost and crying

And Maurice's hand is like an iceberg
Calving its fingers slipping away

Like details on a day
When fog fills the long verandas

And memory wraps each minute
In a mist of blurred vision

And Monique is a shadow
And Maurice is a shadow

And the mirror through the window
Mirrors only fog and shadow

Aspects of Melancholia, the Murderer Pauses

The hand lying on the counterpane
So lightly, the air of the mind
So somber and so gray, the hand
That does not move, lies there
So lightly, as though it were
A ghost, hollowed husk of a hand
Incapable of motion, the hard grasp,
The fist that breaks as it pounds the wall.

The legs that fill slowly with mercury,
That swell in the expansion of the day,
That shrink away to nothing in the night's cold,
The legs that will not move, that are
Stone walls laid loosely near the woods,
Walls that do not tremble in the gale,
That move only down to the waiting soil,
That sink out of sight in the gravity of time.

The heart that beats slowly, the chest
That swells, so slowly, fills and empties
Like a sail in tropical doldrums,
The heart a distant drumming, the empty habit
Of a galley master demanding without hope
That the enslaved oars push the ship
Where the wind does not blow or even hiss,
Blood that lies in the veins without waves.

The air of the mind, so somber and so gray,
No part of the sunlight that passes
Through the window and onto the ceiling,
That forms shadow into blossom, moves silence
Into form, but does not stir the air of the mind,
Lost in gray inertia, lying still in the skull
As a hand of fog, legs of bedrock, lungs shallow
As the scratched grave of a victim, used and laid away.

The Great Dream of Henri Rousseau

It had, of course, to do with angels
And greenery and animals and the beast
We name War so we will not see it is ourselves.

It had, of course, to do with trees,
Their tops like ferns, bark as smooth
As the inside of Clémence's thigh.

It had, of course, to do with the one steel tower
That stands in every dream, and the jungle's
Fur, its swift embrace, obscure surprise.

From copybook and copied art, from the window
Or out the open door, the dream took its source,
Its timid sources like the Loire or Seine.

From the dream you had last night,
Tossing so hard you tugged the sheet loose,
It found a shadow or an elephant's eye.

It has, of course, to do with today,
Dawn light that tugged the sky awake,
Sun's sink into fire and far.

Or, tomorrow, last week, the day after
The last day's sullen pout,
Tiger that missed the buck's quick back.

Worried at the end about Robert's
Breaking the tall tower, he stepped then
Into the greater dream, did not come back.

A flicker browses in the shag of grass
By the curving walk, a vole only a shimmer
Just beyond, the dream asleep.

Thick children like stumps or toadstools
Squat down by the highway, their parents
Aghast, the leopard in the tree.

Under the sea, black submarines ping
And stalk in the green occluded light,
Waiting for the dream to begin to end.

The jungle crept through Paris
Not unlike a war, an army, a fevered lion,
Under the arm of peace, the faces of the great.

Old men stare at each other across the waves,
The jungle grubs their blank dumb eyes,
The dream like an initial press report.

Henri, Henri, the candles dripped on your head,
You paint the face of stars, remember,
Remember the hot wax, red flowers, words of the song.

It has, of course, to do with the world,
Sliding on magma, grinding down, spouting up,
Desert of an old month's nightmare.

Touch the strings with the bow,
Let's go to the fair, look up in the air,
Climb the tower to the very top.

The big cat pauses, looks around,
The gypsy sleeps, the sofa goes to seed,
The piper plays the tune we all can hum.

Yawn, wake up, raise your head, an arm,
Step out to the side, step into the day,
Flicking beak, mouse-run, the blaze.

It had, of course, to do with angels,
With Rousseau's ascent, trumpet's gape,
Held hand, day's pop behind him like a squib.

It has to do with angels, wing's breath
Against the heat, the sudden light,
Great dream that opens up, at last, all sight.

21 May 1984
140th birthday of H. Rousseau

Poe at the End

October. Poe in Baltimore. Poe
At the end, going North, away
From Virginia, keeping promises
Despite the black beak of despair,
Laid over, waiting for the train,
But just now, drunk, out of the coop,
Leaning in Lombard Street
Against the window of a store,
Making his pitched and stammered way
Toward Cooth & Sergeant's Tavern—
(Sergeant Major Poe, First Artillery,
Honorably discharged so many years ago)—
Slow way of starts and fits,
The drink and drugs sluing his heart
Into blind staggers and sways.

Away from Virginia and toward
Virginia in the grave. She played
The harp that January night and sang,
It was a good song, too,
But so soon, so quickly a tiny vessel
Popped in her throat like a New Year's squib
Just as she reached for her last high note.
And for five years it broke and broke
Again, until she died, was laid away,
And Poe learned an awful truth:
Helter skelter or catcher in the rye,
Art kills as often as it saves.

On Lombard Street in Baltimore, memory
Twists him, presses his forehead against the glass,
His heart wheezing like wind through the cottage wall
In Fordham where Virginia lay. His heart lifts
In his chest, flaps clumsily aloft
Like a great white bird, then settles back,
And Poe is grounded, left in the lurch
As he was abandoned by his party friends
After voting all morning under a dozen names:
His own, Usher, Reynolds, Dupin, Pym,

Raising his hand again and again, taking the oath,
Swearing he was who he was and was not,
Swearing he was.

                    Hart Crane asked him
Nearly a century later whether he denied
The ticket, but how could he deny a thing,
He who was all things that day and none,
A multitude of beings and only one,
Leaning on a window, his forehead on the glass,
His eyes unfocused or focused deep within.

And yet he does see past Virginia
With blood on her blouse, past Elmira
Left behind in Richmond, jilted
Before she ever reached the altar,
Past even the bloated face of Edgar Poe
Reflected in the window, drawn and drawn out
In the wobbly glass, the sodden man
In a stranger's threadbare clothes
With only Dr. Carter's borrowed cane
Still clutched in that familiar hand,
Sees through the tortured glass
To a display of pewter and silver
Laid out within the shop, slick knives
With thin images of a singular man
Upon each blade, rounded shining cups
With a bulge-nosed alien face
In each curved surface, two large
Silver plates with his own desperate stare
Reflected plain in each, the brow,
The carved-out cheeks, blue lips
Beneath the sad mustache.

                    But he
Looks beyond this olio of images,
These hard lies and harder truths
Displayed before him, to find
A large silver coffee urn, beknobbed
And crusted with handles and thick
Vines, blossoms and twisted ribbons,
Its surface flat and curved and rounded,
Concave, convex, and convolute,

And in its turbulent reflections
He sees a young man's face,
A young man with dark hair
And uneven eyes, a young man
Leaning on a cane with promises
To keep, a face he recognizes
But cannot name, knows but cannot claim,
That looks him steadily eye to eye.

His heart will soon calm down enough
For him to stutter on, reach Cooth &
Sergeant's, fall onto a bench, be found,
Be carried to the hospital, lie there in fever,
Call Reynolds' name, ease out of delirium
Only to say, gently, "Lord help my poor soul,"
And die, having for one moment on Lombard Street
Learned still another awful truth:
Pell mell or waiting just to die,
Art saves as often as it kills.

Frankenstein's Attic

With the bride locked safely from all help,
Henry, the groom, and Victor bolt to the stairs
Following the monster's muffled moan.
The worried faithful butler trails behind.
They rummage down the second-story hall.
Henry, to the left, casts only a glance
Toward the first door, overturns a chair
In the second room (a tidy parlor
With a long-dead lady's portrait on the wall),
Crosses then to Victor and the butler,
Not pausing by the propped broom, the mop,
The enigma of the tilted empty picture frame,
Circles a broken chair through excelsior
Strewn on the floor, before running
Back again, follows the groan like a faulty beacon
Down to the cellar with its tuns and dusty bottles
Packed in straw.
              But what if we were to stay
With that unnamed retainer in his formal clothes,
Slightly balding, puffing from the exertion,
To climb the stairs at the rear of the set,
Twisting back over the hall, narrow, forgotten,
Seldom used, up and over and into the attic,
Under the steep gables, slanted light standing
In the warped glass of the small windows,
Dust underfoot, and the soft puff of our feet
On the uneven floor, what would we find?

Henry's great-grandmother's stacked hatboxes,
A wicker pram, his cradle under a draped shroud,
Rows of the Baron's discarded shoes, the toes
Bent up in mute salute, a battered chemistry set
Lightly scented with sulphur, a set of golf clubs,
The woods cracked and dry, a lone lightning rod
On three bent feet, two stiff moths in its glass ball,
Never once attached to the steep manor roof,
The stone passage of the main chimney to the sky,
Air as tight as stored bulbs waiting for a new life to come.

But, possibly we would find nothing at the top
Of those steep stairs, only moving shadows
Like those of the searchers on the walls,
Or perhaps just a painted flat, the shoes, the clubs,
The hats and chimney, the chemistry set,
The pram in the dust, and even the steady light,
Only an illusion, a two-dimensional camera trick
Like all the other shadows on the screen—
Henry's memories and dreams that fill the house,
Elizabeth, the Baron, orange blossoms under glass,
The wedding guests, the slapping dancers in the street,
The monster at the window down below.

The monster came to know too late
How everything can suddenly go flat,
Deflate or just as suddenly swell up
Like a tumor or a broken fist,

How the dummy you toss from the windmill
May be your maker, or the flower you seek
To float sinks like a little girl
Or a woman choking back a final scream.

The lesson of the attic is the lesson
Of the film, how the closer we look
The less we see, how the more we think
To know, the less we are able to do,

How the more deeply we explore
The more confused we become,
Until we settle back, decide
To wait for the comfort of the end:

The moment when we will see from afar
The world made whole, and learn
For the very first time the monster's name
And then remember finally our own.

On First Looking into Lawrence Becker's
Reciprocity: Speculations on the Truth
and Falsity of a Sentence

1.1 *The text*

Begins with a definition: 'extended epigraph',
Which you will find (so far) in no other book:
"Story, parable, aphorism or anecdote . . . a moral."

And later, as the argument begins to wind or unwind,
The words extend themselves into the page, the page
Into the book, the reader finds the first of these:

It ends, "He is a fool," which gives the careful reader
Pause, causes (in this case) him to paw deep into the book,
To look for source and analogue, note or demand.

And yet, he does proceed, reads on, finds still another
Anecdote (or tale), this one the brief account of a group
Of friends who lunch together day by day and of the rules

They have developed week by week or year by year,
Unspoken rules (yet understood) of placement, of behavior,
Discourse, speech and sight and sound, of getting on.

This tale tells all, even to the ill-at-ease demeanor
Of random guests who do not recognize the game or even that
It's being played, who stay on, catch on or fail to come again.

And then this sentence, my text particular, occurs:
"In fact, if any of its rules were ever written down
(which will never happen) that one would be in blood."

It is that sentence we must attempt to comprehend.
So much depends upon those words: the text, the text's
Relation to the world we know, the reader's status as mere fool.

2.1 *The fact*

Is that the phrase 'In fact'
Appears to function in the tale
And in the sentence as a sign

That the sentence and the tale
Are true, that facts are facts.

My friend the atomist once said
(Logical atomist, of course;
No physicist would agree)
With Wittgenstein, "The world
Is everything that is the case,"

And then went on to add,
"What is the case, the fact,
Is the existence of atomic facts."
It seemed to me so clear
(This was very long ago).

I know the atomists backed down
Or stepped away, the thing
Collapsing in the harsh bull dose
Of positive assurance
(Yet another Viennese imposture),

And my case, in fact, will seem
Quite insecure if I depend
Only on the *Tractatus*
Or make Whitehead and Russell
My solid ground, my fact,

But still, even if Ludwig
Did cease to make a sound,
Lord Russell got involved
With other kinds of atomic
Deeds, and Alfred drifted

Into the nexus and on to God,
Nevertheless, the phrase
'In fact' hooks all the rest
Of that troubling sentence
To the world, to what it is.

So that, and let's ignore
The 'if' and its result
And just examine the prediction
Cupped in those parentheses—
'(which will never happen)':

"In fact," it says, which means
As I take it, 'in the world',
The rules or any one of them

Written in the tangle of arteries
And veins, written in the blood's dance
Across the eye, in the dragtime
Of the ear, written without rime,
Without reason, blood's rule,
Blood's absolute authority,
Blood's reign that floods the heart,
Drains in the rhythm of the wrist,
And feeds the brain, red thoughts,
The logic, the fact, and the red, red dream.

2.3 *The speculations*

Have to do with the ways of words,
Their doings in the world, undoings
Of the world, text and context,
The placing of "the rational man,"
The contract that makes us all
Seek out a place in which to stand
As we utter the words that draw
The world's confusions into place,
That place, the place in which we stand:

Does the writing of the rules
That can never be written
Negate the text in which they are written
In a reciprocal arrangement
Or disarray of truth and lie,
Of truth discovered where truth lies?

Or does the writing of the rules
And the writing that they cannot be written
Pulse on the page, a blood pact
That none can read without confusion?

Or does the truth lie in the recognition,
In the metacognition that leads us
To understand that our relation to the page
Transcends the world of fact that lies
On the page, leads us to know
That the rules cannot be written
In the world that lies on the page
But may be written in the world
In which that page lies?

And what, then, of the fact that a reader
May recognize himself or herself
As one of the members of the group
And thus may read the rules of that world
In this world and also recognize them
As the unwritten rules of this world
Now written here, although disguised?

Like Pilate must we cry out, "What
Is truth?" and wash our hands
And thereby nail truth and the word
To the hard tree of deadly fact,
Our surrender written nowhere
And everywhere for all time in blood?

3.1 *The moral*

Lies beyond the rules, the words
About the rules, the words about
The words about the rules,
The words about the words
About the words about the rules,
And so on in an infinity of iteration,
The ordered chaos of repetition
Toward which our speculations
Must finally incline, decline
Or recline, lie down to die,
Tire but never end, end over end.

The truth is that language lies
In order to be true, imagined
Truth of rhythm and surprise,
A lover's lie, a play of words
Like the dance of atoms
In eternally recomposing fact,
The fool's wisdom that knows
The world is everything that is
And more, that knows the turbulence
Of blood, the fractal beauty
Of disarray, the reciprocity
Of truth and truth and truth
And truth, the word within
The world within the word,
World and word without end.

Understanding George Garrett: The Movie

A window:

It opens in
So that we see: not sunlight
Or blusters of snow
Or high water rising,
But rather:
Beyond the casement,
The sill specked with bird droppings,
Feathers, a sprinkle of dead flies,
Past the cobweb winking upper left,
Our eyes moving like the camera
In a Hitchcock film,
Crane shot, intrusion
Into a privacy where we will discover
A startling truth about ourselves
And just possibly survive
To tell the tale,
There: he is:
Stalled, staring at a calendar on the wall,
The floor strewn with a yellow litter of paper
As if the first ragged forsythia
Of an early spring he once imagined
Had exploded around him
But left him unharmed:
He is making a novel,
An Elizabethan metafiction,
Barfoote, Marlowe's death, Hunnyman,
Women who laugh and show their teeth:
Or he is attempting to make a poem
With a window in it
That opens out
Into the raging world
So that we can finally see
As we are seen.

A memory:

Cannot be trusted,
No more than can a photograph,
Her hand lingered fondly over a print,
Collar cocked behind her neck,
His grin as he sits upon a desk,
Cigarette in his hand
(Which dates the shot),
My photograph on the concrete wall,
A book of photographs
Tipped in and labeled in white ink:
Florida, the living room, the *José Gaspar,*
The drowsing alligator in the park,
Mother, father, son, pages
Of lost friends,
Or printed in a book:
Boxer, graceful dancer,
The delicacy of her guitar,
Florida, Vienna, Rome,
The children staring at the lens,
All blurred as through a window in the·rain,
My memories confused with yours,
Yours with his,
The story you told me (or was it him?)
About the Studebaker and your Uncle Ned,
The Studebaker I remember on a foggy night
With the generator light blinking YES,
Blinking YES, blinking YES,
(Or was it NO?),
The story he told me
About his uncle the dancer
And Fred Astaire,
Her eyes as blue as a bright Celtic afternoon
Or the way she props her notebook on her knees,
Her glasses on her nose,
Stories that happened or did not
Or will, or never will, bird on a tree limb,
Rider headed south from Scotland,
Keys clattering on a ring,
Shame, humiliation, disgrace,
Blade that pierces an eye like a beam:
Memories that float like scum on a pond

Or wisps of cloud on a late spring day,
Your presence in the room
When you are far away,
His voice on the phone
Asking me if I remember,
If I recall, my voice
Asking him the name, the date,
The weather, the score,
The punchline of the joke,
Sure that he will know,
His memory photographic,
Will remember the way,
Will know exactly where she is,
Will tell me who you are
And just who and where I am.

A door:

To the theater
Where *The Playground* is playing,
: To the den
Where *The Young Lovers*
Is on the television screen,
: To the dorm room
Where puzzled sophomores
Are watching *Frankenstein*
Meets the Space Monster
And wondering why,
: To my study
Where I was supposed
To write an essay
On the screenplays of George Garrett
But didn't,
: That bulged on the big screen
In Charlottesville
On a cold day in January
When we thought *The Haunting*
Was making us shake in our coats
But it was really only
An open emergency exit
That was letting winter in,
: That shuts forever in a poem

By Borges, or opens
In a longer poem
Of Robinson's,
: That edges slowly open
Or slaps shut
When you whisper the word *adore*
Into her ear,
: That slammed to keep you out
In the house where no one lives,
: That you broke open
With an ax in a movie
By Kubrick, or possibly a teleplay
By Bergman,
: To the past, : to the future,
: To Paradise,
: To Hell,
: Complete with lady, tiger,
Christie Brinkley, Helen Vendler,
: To the tomb that Poe's Irene
Threw stones at, poor child of sin,
Thrilling to think it was the dead
Who groaned within,
: To our just reward,
Or that opens just in time
To mercy's plea,
: That is marked DANGER,
: That says COME IN,
: To the projection booth
Where the reel falters
Then stammers like a locomotive wheel,
Begins,
The projectionist leaning
On the window sill,
Stiff flies under his elbows,
To see a burst of yellow blossoms
Fill the screen in perfect focus,
A crane shot up and back,
Slow pan, and then crane down
To : a window : that opens in
To : a memory :
Where : a door : swings slowly wide
To reveal your best friend,
In his hand a red pen,

Hard at work on a novel
Or a poem, or perhaps a film
That opens in springtime,
Hawk high in the April wind,
Forsythia in ragged bloom,
From window and door
Its glow illuminates the room,
Close shot: the hand, the pen,
The remembered rhythm of words
Steady across the yellow page.

Florida

Noticing how Hitchcock sketches in
Another place, quickly, obviously,
Makes it there by insisting that
It is there,

(Scotland: a kilt, sheep of course,
The Flying Scotsman, stone bridges,
The great Forth Bridge, hymn book,
Long-haired cows, rushing burns,
Bare mountains brushed with clouds)

(Or, the Swiss: their yodels, clocks,
Chocolates in silver foils, bells, bowls,
A lake that echoes and echoes the Alps)

         I propose to assert
The existence of Florida as simply,
Using only a boy's distant memory
As source:

                Green shadows, bamboo
In the corner of the yard, the banana tree
Just outside the small kitchen window,
Rain that rises and falls each bright afternoon,
Lily pads so thick on the bay's water
That you feel you could walk all the way out
To the white yachts, the *José Gaspar*
Docked black just down the street,
A field of eggplants, swollen and purple
As far as you can see, papayas,
The juice sweet and worth begging for,
The rattle and ricochet of spoken Spanish
Too quick for your ear, Spanish moss
Bearding the ancient trees, coconuts
That crack the ground, the Royal Palm,
White Palm Beach suits, everyone tanned
Except the new tourists who drift across
The sloped bridges like awful ghosts,
Who wait for the open ones to lower
As caught eels squirm by their feet
Toward the narrowing gap, the small

Startled alligator who opens his mouth
And hisses like an opossum away from home
As you explore the adventitious roots
Of the banyan, a dark maze, wide and deep,
You venture in, the air barred and thick,
As day seeps out through the close limbs
Until you are only a pale glimmer, an echo,
A wink of white cloth, a shimmer of youth,
A brush of quick light, and are gone.

A Dream of Uncles

I have been blessed with uncles
Who took me hunting for squirrel
And for crows, who shovelled
The stiff hound into the hole
I helped dig, who rode with me
In the bed of the truck, tilted
In a cane-bottomed chair, showed
Me the rhythm of words on a page,
Let me ramble the bookshelves,
Palmed a silver dollar into my hand
For no reason other than I was there.

The wisdom of uncles, their advice
Like silver on a day crowded with crows,
Black beaks, ruffed necks, black claws,
Caws scattering the silence into shards
Of cracked glass; like silver which warms
To the touch quickly, is valuable
In exchange, shines like caught water
Catching light by desert palms.

My dead uncle Clifton who died young,
So mysterious, only a silver shadow
In an album, a headstone, and now
So many uncles dead; let me name
The living: Grant and Letcher,
Basil and George, all of them alive,
And all my uncles grinning in photographs,
Lounging against each other, shy,
Ducking their heads, ready to break free,
Move away from the Kodak's click.

Last night I dreamed of cats, the dream book
Warns of treachery in those close,
Cats playing, leaping, stretching their claws,
The black cat strikes like lightning,
But my uncles were there as well,
Predicting prosperity, Uncle Carroll
As silent and relaxed as one of his cows
Answering to her name, and Kenner, Charlie,
Wilbur well again, the boy who should

Not have lived but did, all my other uncles
In other rooms, just beyond the open door.

These are only names to you, but perhaps
You'll understand what I mean, what a dream
Of uncles really means, even if I don't
Spell it out: a gray day, nothing stirs,
The crow's black eye foretells the night,
Claws swell from the black cat's paws,
Your shoulders will not lift, betrayed,
You are ready to cry uncle, give in;
It is then that you have a dream of uncles,
A house full of uncles, uncles lolling
On the porch steps, uncles in bed,
Uncles napping on the sofa, your uncle
Passing silver over your palm, the future
In your hands, it glints like dawn,
A breeze stirs the bare branches
And crows burst into something like a song.

Blue Monk

Moves up by half steps,
Every sharp and flat in play,
Much like the day Nellie complained
That all the pictures in the house were crooked,
Straightened them herself just that morning,
Each one tilted differently, no two alike.

He's still around, back in town
On tape and disc, on the VCR,
Monk's music, Monk's mumble,
His foot tilted, moving up and down
Just like the notes, played
Two keys side by side at once,
Looking for the quarter tones,
The notes that were not there.

Miles complained that you couldn't play with the man,
Those queer chords, broken rhythms
Gave you nothing on which to stand,
No straight lines, everything bent out of shape.
Well, you needn't, but you should.

Finger it out, note by note,
Makes your ear strain, finger falter,
Stammer on the keys, and yet it is all,
As they say, so inevitable.

Monk confessed that he pushed the pictures
Off kilter himself. Take note of that.

Ornette

takes care of the sounds

knows that music should be played
the way it goes not
the way it was supposed to go

that bars enclose as well
as protect or support

that keys can lock you in
as well as open doors

remembers when all
some people knew was that he played
a plastic sax that
his music could not be listened to

knows now that everyone knows
it was music that could not be heard
yet

said once to Cherry LaFaro Higgins Dolphy
Hubbard Haden Blackwell let's try
to play the music and not the background

knows that freedom feels like chaos
without the strange attractor of the heart

that melody creates harmonies
virgin beauty follows lonely
woman not necessarily
the other way around

that the key is all in pitch
that voice is all that form is
ordered chaos sense is sound

said once that every passage of music has a place
to
stop

A Postcard from Bruges

1914. The British Seventh Division
Lands at Zeebrugge, moves out to Brugge,
October. "The girls pinched our cap badges
For souvenirs." The road from Oostende
To Brugge. They settle for grilled sardines.
Not a shot has yet been fired. A good war.
The girls pinch their cap badges, etc.
"A good war so far." Not a shot.
Flat country, a canal. The girls pinch.
Good war. Not a shot has been fired.

1944. This time it is the Canadians
In September. Like the situation
On the western front, the firing goes on
Night and day. Churchill to Smuts: "I like
The situation." Crossing rivers, canals.
Only 2,400 out of 10,000 make it back
Across the river at Arnhem in October.
"Can Hitler last?" Not a girl in sight.
The soldiers pinched between canals
Like sardines in a tin. Night and day.

1991. "Chocolate is everywhere." Americans
Come in September by jetfoil from London
To eat chocolate and clams, to eat
Belgian waffles. Their teeth are shot
With sugary residue. Packed like sardines
Into the motorcoach, girls pinch themselves
To see if they're awake. They cross canals
Calmly. They like this situation,
Their travels. They like us. They think
Of us often, send this postcard from Bruges.

Just Now, Some Things in Common

But isn't there something in common about zebras and cows? An ostrich and a hyena.

—Charles Fort

And something in common, too, about the way
The air this morning is textured with autumn
And the rusty sweat on the brow
Of the metal statue of Lenin swinging
From a crane in some small park or the other
In Riga? Or the way the Ukrainian flag
Resembles an Easter display in your favorite
Department store in the mall
And the look of disbelief on the face
Of the teenager in Philadelphia who captured
A ball in play and thought it was his for life?

We need Fort back to straighten it out for us,
To enable us to see how the plumes
Billowing over the strong muscles of those bare legs
And the cackling grin of gut-eating *fisi*
Are one and the same, and to explain again
The zebra's willingness to plow with the cow.

Kadare stares out a slick window at the rain
Across the operatic rooftops of Paris
While Nabokov begins a fairly complicated joke
Designed to get a laugh from Pushkin in Paradise.
The zebra skips away from the hyena's jaws
Into a zoo in Albuquerque under the waning moon:
The cow and the ostrich are one.

Unions march like Ukrainians on the Mall,
Sing "Solidarity Forever," the umpire starts the game
As Labor Day crowds throng the malls, the air
Sweetens, and, just now, Lenin *né* Ulyanov falls.

Brain Power

Tonight they are showing off
For the TV cameras tidily wrapped brains,
Tucked in stiff white paper,
Neatly folded, taped in place,
Not just any brains, but shelves
Of Soviet brains, preserved for research
In a locked cabinet, taken out
On occasion and sliced like cheese
Or, to continue the comparison,
The fine thin slices of corned beef
A good deli can supply.

Lenin's brain has been here for years,
Revolution still in its lobes and bulbs,
Peeled slowly away thought by thought,
And Stalin's hard gray brain as well.

Just think of those two hollow heads
Once upon a time, lying side by side
In a crowded tomb in Red Square,
Safely sealed in glass
Lest the winds from the steppes
Whistle audible disharmony
Through their ears.

This is Stalin's collection, they say,
His great idea, this collection of brains,
And, as evidence of the final grant given to artists
Who live off the state, trust the state,
Cut to: the paper packets on the shelf
Marked Mayakovsky and Gorky and Eisenstein,
A montage sequence of brains and wax casts
Of brains, Lenin, Stalin, Gorky, maybe Sakharov,
Poets, thugs, thinkers, all meat for the blade.

You might think, too, of Jeremy Bentham,
Snug in a locked cabinet in London,
A wax head on his shoulders,
His real head, shriveled and dry
Between his feet, a useful monument
By his own bequest to his brain power,
A plan to make us all pause in awe.

Or the millions of embalmed brains
Planted in American soil, locked in bronze,
Never to sprout into startling bloom.
Is this what it comes to, then?
All the words and deeds, the minds
That frame troubled lyrics, elegant formulae,
And a million sudden deaths?
A package on a shelf, a name
Penciled in grease?

A man dressed in lightning,
Seated in an empty tomb, answers
In a voice abrupt as a knife,
"He is not here. Look,
There is the place where they laid him."

Ecstasy

Et j'entendis une grande voix.
—L'Apocalypse

What roused in Hugo such ecstasy
The day he wrote this poem, caught up,
Staring at the voice beyond the wall?
Or Stein, for that matter,
On a walk in Spain, clapping her hands,
Head tilted back, a magpie
Flat against the backlit sky,
Or Blake, playing at Paradise, naked in the garden,
Did he see, etched above the trees,
Great calipers embrace the day?

Now, for example, all they would likely see
From this window are unpicked fox grapes
Knotted black and hard on a wound vine,
A lone house finch feeding on thistles,
Sunlight broken with branches and leaves.

No golden stars, not a single crown of fire
In this clear air, no sound of distant waves
Bowing on an eternal shore, and yet
Here, in this fractured light, Victor's voice
Still says, *"C'est le Seigneur, le Seigneur Dieu!"*

(*After the French of Victor Hugo*)

Autumn Letter to London

Yes, Julia, London is not home, has a river,
    A great river, to be sure,
But not the Father of Waters, only a sliver,
    Not long though wide and deep
With history echoing along the barges
    And banks like the bells
Of Big Ben (the very name enlarges
    Your sense of who you are,
Of where you really are), Shakespeare
    In conversation with a boatman
Whom, on a sudden whim, he makes steer
    Back up the river to where they began,
Or Turner catching the Parliament fire
    In oil and water, or even Eliot
Dreaming of a gilded barge, a choir
    Of nymphs, a golden past
That never was in just that way.
    It was not home to them
Either, although they did manage to stay
    Longer than you plan to do.
Rumor has it you did see the Queen,
    One of the Little Princesses grown up
Who stood on the palace balcony, were seen
    There braving the bombs of the blitz.
They were the first thing about London
    I noticed, apart from Dick Whittington's cat,
Those little girls looking up and down,
    Then at the camera, waving, brave,
Ignoring the Heinkels high overhead, thick wings
    With bent noses like sharks,
Waved, smiled, were not afraid, flames licking
    At London, fooled only themselves, and us.
No, it is not home. The sun sets
    Almost before it rises.
The cold fogs rise in damp runlets
    That brush your face
Like cold scarves. Think how thick
    And dark they must have been
In coal-fired days: quite a trick
    Just to maneuver down the street,

The gas lamps just yellow blurs
    Filtered through wet wool.
I don't know why all this occurs
    To me just now. London was always
Bright and clear when I was there,
    Young women's legs sunburnt bright
Red all down the backs, like flares
    Along the streets, the fronts
Still white as winter, never thought
    To rotate in the grass
Along the Serpentine, simply sought
    The bright heat you are missing
Now. Maybe it's because it is so cold
    And gray here in Virginia
Today. Even New Orleans broke old
    Records for low temperatures
Last night. Your cat Henrietta
    Must be curled in ball
Or maybe writing you a letter
    The way she used to do
Before the summer skittered away
    Through some hole or the other
Leaving only ice pellets that flay
    The air like a cat-o'-nine-tails.
These are autumn thoughts, winter
    In the air, counting birthdays,
Shocked at the sum, memory bent to
    New tasks, listing, numbering,
Leafing through the past like the album
    I found in my mother's attic
With pictures of the man whose thumb
    Dug into my ear and found dimes—
The Mexican magician who lived down the hall—
    Or the wrestler who tried to teach
Me how to swim, or the Florida fall
    When I started off to school
Where I've stayed ever since, kept
    From graduation by people
Like you, poets whose language leapt
    To make each day new anew.
This year at the college it's all been
    Reports and memos, meetings

That always seem to start, never end
    Until exhaustion sets in.
But no complaints from me. I'm writing
    Poems between appointments,
Teaching Hitchcock, actually delighting
    In the words writers hand
Me to read. Anita, for example, is working
    On a story about the color red,
Another about little boys who are lurking
    Everywhere you'd never think to look,
And even one about a girl who likes
    To count. What more could I ask?
The dog and I scratch fleas, take hikes
    Around the neighborhood, hoping
They'll hop off or freeze along the way;
    The cat's rough tongue seems
To do the job for her. I'd even say
    There was a lesson in that
For us all, but I don't want to believe it.
    Anyway, as I was saying, the memories
Rise in autumn, the past, if you retrieve it,
    Causing, say, you, in my dreams,
To walk on lily pads in Florida, make forays
    Across the long causeway in a jeep,
As in a story by Nabokov or maybe Borges.
    But what does this have to do with London?
Or even home? Perhaps an autumn definition
    Of just what London or Shakespeare
Or home or your cat or mine or my contrition
    At not writing you as I promised
Have in common. Even hot Mercury has ice caps,
    The newspaper noted yesterday.
Cats can be replaced by better mousetraps
    Although they'll seldom purr.
Promises are never kept in just the way
    We planned. The days do grow shorter,
And even the Mississippi, like a Shakespeare play,
    Comes to a satisfying or an ambiguous end
(You deconstruct it as you wish). Still, the
    Promises are kept—like appointments
On a busy day, breathless, willy-nilly,
    With irritation or apology in haste,

But kept. If winter comes, the poet said,
    Can spring be far behind?
And sure enough a purple finch, tipped red
    Along the upper half of its body,
Just landed at my empty feeder to remind me
    That the seed is still in the cellar
And, before spring comes, I should kindly
    Keep my promise, do my job.
So, Julia, I'd better end this letter
    And get to it.
But, a reminder to you: you'd better
    Continue to look both ways
Before you cross a British street,
    Watch winter deepen every day,
Observe, and read the poems of Louis MacNeice,
    Take notice when he says,
"What the wind scatters, the wind saves."
    The wind ruffles the finch's red feathers.
I've got to go. Remember: the love that enslaves
    Us, ties us to the world in ice and fire,
Runs like a river through our days and nights
    From frigid Minnesota to the Gulf,
Wrinkles the frozen sky in fiery northern lights,
    Also ties us together, together or apart.

Secrets

The dignity of movement of an ice-berg is due to only one-eighth of it being above water.

—Ernest Hemingway

*

The ice-blue eye of the tall countess
Holds you like a mounting pin as your whole
Thorax tightens, grows chitinous and hard.

Her muddy left eye wavers, but the blue one
Pins you fast, never blinks, stares you down.

**

He has been standing in the cold rain
For over an hour, his sodden raincoat
Soaked through, heavier on his cold back

Than the weight of papers sealed in oilskin
In his coat pocket, of what they bare.

***

The thought wraps itself around your heart
Like an icy hand, squeezes until you gasp
As sweat presses your brow like cold oil.

You try to walk, but your legs are like air,
They will not bear the weight of this dark thought.

****

She winks and nods her head, light twinkles
In her eyes as though they were electronically
Enhanced, or shining through layers of air

Like stars, as though she knows of things
That have traveled years and transmit power.

*****

The memory that wakes you in the night,
Sits you straight up in bed, reaching for the light
That isn't there, a light in another room,

Another place, another year, the light that failed,
That once left you gasping in the dark,

******

These things you ought to know:

The blue eye is glass and cannot see;
The buyer never came, his faction fell;
Your legs are stronger than you know;
She knows only what is shiny, what is near;
You are like a candle, your light a prayer.

for Anita Thompson

Domestic Cosmology

How soon unaccountable I became tired and sick,
Till rising and gliding out I wander'd off by myself,
In the mystical moist night-air, and from time to time,
Look'd up in perfect silence at the stars.
                                        —Walt Whitman

          Hearing the learn'd astronomer
          Will do that, all those light years,
          Bent light, curved space dented like dough
          Waiting for the oven or bulging
          As the yeast rises, stars, swarms, clusters,
          And just beyond the nearest event horizon,
          A black hole sucking like the vacuum
          Whining in the room next door.

          Why bother? Leave the gas on, light a match
          And blow the whole thing up.
          The neighbors on Alpha Centauri
          Won't even know it for 4.3 years,
          If they're home at all.

          Just sit here and stare at the wall,
          Wonder who's so busy next door,
          Feeling too useless to go and see,
          Not really able to rise and glide
          Out like Walt did, with the night air
          Scarcely moist, no rain for two months.

          And then suddenly—just as the stars
          Actually did last night, in perfect silence
          Through the smoky haze when the cold front
          Passed through, needling everywhere,
          Stuck all over the cushion of night sky—
          The thought comes that the whole cosmos
          May well be tucked like a decorated thimble
          In the corner of God's cluttered sewing box:

          Of course, no heavenly chorus breaks out,
          The day continues, the chores remain, the dog

Needs to be walked, the leaves are piling up
Along the way, and, just as though it matters,
The whole universe appears to be waiting
For something to begin just here, just now.

for Anita Thompson

Winter Letter to Bluefield

The images, Anita, that come to mind
    When you write a letter,
Or when I write one, a rare enough event . . .
    Perhaps I'd better
Explain just what I mean, since meaning
    Is somehow what I think
This will all be about—so, what I mean
    Is just that curious mental kink
Which creates the person you're writing to
    (In this instance, you) clearly in focus
At a particular moment in time's texture
    At a single locus,
That set of all points defined by who you are—
    In your own special case
(Appropriately enough for someone who has asked
    "Who am I?" to herself, face to face)
Two images, twinned, one by actual memory,
    The other by *its* twin, imagination:
The first, memory's gift from the night
    While on a nocturnal peregrination,
Walking the dog across the campus,
    I saw you through lit window glass
Writing a story on solar radiation, oblivious
    To our presence, our shadow pass
Across your field of vision. You were wearing
    Headphones like a wandering solarnaut,
Listening, I suppose, to some kind of music
    And, whether hearing it or not,
Swaying to its rhythm as though to a spring breeze
    Or the virtual music of the spheres.
I was not spying, I assure you, no Peeping Tom
    No matter how it appears,
Just the dog and I walking by, looking in
    But knowing you were not there,
Even though I could see your face, your eyes
    Deep within the luminescent screen, elsewhere,
Radiant, streaming out from the sun,
    Sailing, to quote myself, on solar wind.
The other image of you in my mind today
    Is formed of fancy and a blend

Of place names, weather reports, and long novels
        That take place in other places
(Usually by British authors, theologians and scholars
        With disheveled hair and longish faces).
To begin with, the air here is bright and clear
        (A perfect day, for that matter, to walk the dog),
But I hear on the TV news report that Bluefield
        Should expect freezing rain or snow, fog
That will not lift all day. No surprise then
        That I should see you there
In a Bluefield of the mind, a place that's always
        Colder than it is here or anywhere
Nearby, a place that's split in broken mountains,
        That glows an eldritch icy blue
Even though I know that it does not (I have visited
        Or, at least, driven through),
But just now I picture you, walking (or maybe drifting)
        Across a wide and snowy field
(A blue field I would have said but for the pun),
        Pressing through icy twigs and branches that do not
        yield
Until you say the proper words in the proper way.
        You are wearing your red corduroy jacket
(The one I complimented) and your golden leggings,
        Following an echo, knowing you can track it
Through the cold confusion to its distant source.
        Do you see my problem, then?
How do I write a letter to such a person—
        An artist lost in space and solar wind
In real time and, at once, that mythic explorer
        Lost in rimed Bluefield and the swirling time
Of my imagination? Small wonder that I seldom write
        Letters, my personal sin or crime,
The one that one day will do me in and leave me all alone,
        Finally abandoned by all my friends,
Left to an empty house, an empty room, an empty mailbox,
        Empty head, too, probably, all my just ends.
But I won't brood about my deserts, fair or unfair,
        Just now. After all, I *am* writing to you,
Or both of you, and by now I should be used to double
        vision.
        Think of that photo in which I'm split in two,

The one in the coffee-table book: Julia is telling
    Us the tale, has everyone's attention
But yours (you're staring off as if to the sun
    Or nearby planets), but I guess I should mention
That you're actually thinking of how you'll extend
    The story when the turn is yours (you're next),
And I'm there, too, chin in hand, looking right at her
    As she spins the tale, relaxed, unvexed,
At ease, but in the mirror there I am, too,
    Looking right at you. In time present,
Listening to Julia tell the story; in time future,
    In the mirror, caught in the pleasant
Occupation of watching you create the story
    Yet to come. It would take Einstein
Or at least Alice through her looking glass to work out
    The equations for your time, mine,
Even Julia's in that scene—all together, all apart,
    All over the place, time bent and refracted,
Scattered and bowed like light through a prism,
    Compressed, intense, let loose, protracted.
And isn't that the way the moment always seems—
    Singular, bifurcated, trifurcate, multiform?
Or, for that matter, the way it has always seemed:
    Whether Heraclitus insisting that the norm
Is always abnormal, the only lasting thing
    That nothing ever lasts, or the astrologer
(Say, Ptolemy or even Paracelsus) who saw
    The planets as a kind of celestial college or
Gathering of the wise, guiding our days
    And nights, in concord or having fights
Among themselves (like any college faculty)
    With the students (us) forced to pay the price.
And what makes it worse, depending on the moment
    Of our first cries in this world,
The lessons are different for us, each and each,
    Relativity displayed, revealed, unfurled:
Uranus ignites Mars, or Mars contacts the Sun,
    Saturn is in retrograde,
Beware of heavy machinery, or, be bold;
    All decisions must be weighed
Against the celestial sway and shove
    Of the planets' every even move.

I know your friend the learn'd astronomer
        would disapprove
Of my mentioning the truths of the astrologers,
        But even he must admit they taught
And teach us the rules of change, the rule
        Of instability, the flux that ought
To set us free to move but is too often
        The thing we fear (you and I) the most,
That freezes us to the spot, that makes us stoics
        Daring nothing, our only boast
That we cannot lose that which we do not have.
        (But, then, of course, we've lost
Everything before we ever had it, and that
        Seems a dreadful cost
To pay for such minor peace of mind.)
        So, Anita, this is my best attempt.
To write a letter to a double-visioned you;
        Chaotic, in order, in control, unkempt,
It is rather like our conversations.
        The day is passing. The cold blue sky,
Clear as a field of ice, is burning to a fiery point
        Of red and gold. I've got to try
To bring things in this letter to a point as well.
        (But when does a poem really ever
Have a point other than itself? All day,
        All night in the atmosphere, never
Being other than its complex, duplicitous self.)
        But I did claim that it has to do
With meaning, so I will try my best
        To leave at least a clue
To what it's (or I'm) about. I've been reading
        George Barker, his words, his thought, his
Vision, who says, "The mystery of the world is this:
        That we do not know what is."
Alone we are born (even twins), the truism says,
        And, our secrets with us, alone we die.
But we are never truly alone at our loneliest,
        Feeling the moon's tug in its passage by,
Knowing the sweep of cosmic dust in our veins,
        Swaying to a music we cannot hear,
Exploring a landscape of despair with only the echo
        Of an echo in our ears.

The images that come to mind, perhaps these are
    The substance of this letter,
Any letter, even those Walt Whitman found
    In the street from God, the weather
Of God's mind on every page, the "kosmos" itself.
When you try to identify just who you are,
Always remember that the answer is never simple,
    That it depends on the placement of the viewer,
That a photo of the universe from just the right angle
    Might well reveal your features in the stars
And in the empty spaces in between, Alpha Centauri,
    Sirius, the Crab Nebula, Venus, Mars,
A tree of galaxies flowing from your hair,
    The red and gold explosion of the sun
Warming the icy cold of empty space with solar wind.
    And one more thing before I'm done:
It is true we lose the things we hold dearest
    But equally true that because we hold them dear
We find ourselves which we otherwise had lost,
    Find ourselves whole—just now, just here.

You Told Me

That October will soon come to this town
For the first time, that the first
Slick posters for a concert will appear
Overnight on its walls and kiosks,
That for the first time an errand boy
Will deliver your bills to you,
That winter steep in snow will arrive
For the first time, and that a young man
Will tell a woman, "I will wait for you
At 6:15 on the corner by the Post Office."
No one will ever know
Just who he will be.

That is what you told me.

You told me something else, too,
A secret I will never tell,
But you did not know that even then
I was walking the sidewalks of this town,
That I was coming to love this town,
That I want to be caught here
In a sudden rain, that I want to huddle
Under the eaves of a building
With a wet, stirring crowd,
That I want to catch sight of you,
A quick glimpse of red in the rain,
Coming as always from far away,
That I want to cross the street
And be suddenly beside you,
My hand touching your shoulder,
That you will look up
And say, "I have been working,"
But that you will also say,
"I have been looking for you
All over for the last four hours."

And I wonder whether you will really
Say those words to me, or whether
You have already forgotten them.

(*After the Albanian of Ismail Kadare*)

Spring Letter to Paradise

It is, mother, Groundhog Day today,
    Scarcely the first day of spring,
But spring has been in the steep play
    Of light across varied weather,
In the way the birds flit and glide
    By the window, the way the cat
Crouches, switches her tail, begins to slide
    Across the floor to the open door,
A bright day portending six more weeks
    Of bleak winter, just as it did
Last year, a day that always speaks
    Some sort of truth to those
Who listen well. No more winter
    For you then, weeks for us,
For though I found you at the center
    Of life's great mystery,
Still in bed, tucked in, quiet, cold
    As the winter we had yet to live,
You were gone, ninety-one years old,
    "Passed," as Lelani put it,
And what was the last small thing I said
    The night before, "Good night"
Or "Good-bye," before you were dead
    And passed away, gone over, gone?
No matter now. We always liked
    Groundhog Day, its air of prophecy,
Until the actual passage of hours spiked
    Its mystery and turned it into time.
A good day to go, then, all things finally
    Resolved, everything we doubt and fear
And hope made clear, all questions kindlily
    Answered, no secrets, face to face.
If I were to speculate about Paradise, I know
    I'd get it completely wrong,
But I hope there's a place to go
    Or be where with any luck
You can catch Miles and Monk playing
    Together in perfect harmony,
The quarter tones all there, saying
    It's all right to Charles Ives

In the audience, who nods his approval.
    And maybe that is the truth
Or at least truth on the slant, one removal
    Or two from something totally different,
Totally the same. But here it isn't spring,
    Though spring is on the way, the hyacinths
I planted after your funeral beginning
    Already to appear, green tips
Above the grass, yet still and cold
    In the frigid air today, waiting
For the next warm day, hopeful, bold,
    Neither doubt nor fear bred in the bulb,
As sure of resurrection as Apollo was
    When he planted them in the Greek myth.
A doubled day, then, not far from Christmas,
    Not too much farther to Easter,
Both winter and spring, twinned
    As you sometimes thought I was in your last years,
The nice little boy playing with clothespins,
    Making roadways under the table,
And the graying man with broken eyes,
    A grin as crooked as your arthritic hands,
Saying, "No, there's only me, hard as I try,"
    A whisper of white in a banyan tree
Reflected and lost for a time in our conversation.
    And aren't we all more than we seem,
A community of selves in complex relation,
    All with the same name, often estranged?
Anita is just now claiming that she is six
    Different people at least, and I
Lost count some time ago of my own odd mix
    Of selves imagined, selves constructed,
Selves injured and healed, lost and found again.
    To have them all one, freed of the rule
Of stars and planets, of death and sin,
    Of time and loss and shame, that must
Be Paradise, no matter how we dream it here.
    No, it is not spring, the tree branches
Knotted like old bones, the new buds near
    But still sealed in the dogwood
You planted with your own hands, the one
    I'll have to sell soon along with the house

Where you lived for over forty years, the sun
    Luring the cat to the window,
But not warming the day. The house is silent,
    Anita and Julia are far away. Only time
Is moving in this quiet beauty, violent
    And destructive, wearing away everything
We care for, emptying us into a lonely grave.
    And yet . . . in your voice . . . light
Sings along the glass: *what we truly wish to save*
    We must give away; what we truly wish to keep
We must surrender; what we love will be ours
    Forever. "There is that in me,"
This is Walt Whitman (on my mind today for hours),
    "I do not know what it is—
But I know it is in me." And I know, too,
    How it moves along the soul like light
Along the windowpane, leads me to go to
    Seek the day, to find the open door
To Paradise just here, to know to
    Answer the promptings of the heart,
Know for the first time what we all really owe to
    Each other, the debt each day repays.

Loading a Shoebox

With scraps, stuffing it
Tight, bits of paper
With instructions to look
In the glove compartment,
Three lines of a poem
Given to you in a dream,
A message you found
On your answering machine
That makes your flesh crawl,
Skin creep, three tissues,
Three separate kisses,
Your annoyance at a day
Filled with betrayal
And true understanding,
A handstand in a cold corner,
A handshake, a handsaw,
A hawk (you can tell
The difference), this day,
Another day like every day
Like no other.

Ou sont ilz, ou, Vierge souvraine?

That the snow that blows today,
A scattering of light, a twist
Of defined wind, will last the day.

That the smile in your mirror,
Open and gentle, does not conceal
Sorrow like a secret river.

That, in veined time's
Turbulent eddies and whorls,
Our hands will ever touch.

That the universe itself,
That dusting of scattered light,
Even has boundaries, has an edge.

These are doubts.
Doubt them not.

That no one will ever remember
This snow that teases the jay's
Ruffed back, will even remember today.

That we will forever keep our secret
Selves secret lest we lose each other
And so losing lose ourselves.

That, no matter how sure the day,
No matter how, the first time
Our hands touch will be the last.

That the coiled circle of the universe
Is rimmed with light and empty shadow,
Itself the edge of nothing.

These are fears.
Fear them.

That this snow will drift into memory
Flecked with red and gold feathers,
Will gleam in sunset like a great dream.

That one day we will trade secrets
Face to face, that you will recognize
Them as I shall as one and the same.

That I shall one day take your hand,
Perhaps in Paradise or just here, just now,
And find it is my own.

That the edge of the universe will stretch
And knock like the thin blue shell of an egg
As something stretches its new damp wings.

These are hopes.
Hope for them.

1984– 1992 S.D.G.